BAKE IT HAPPEN

Why Your **Oven is HOT**
But Your **Margins are NOT,**
And How To **Fix It**

BAKE IT HAPPEN

Why Your **Oven is HOT**
But Your **Margins are NOT,**
And How To **Fix It**

ABHEY GOYAL

Available on amazonkindle

Worldwide Published by

Pendown Press
PREMIUM BUSINESS PUBLISHER

PENDOWN PRESS LLP

An ISO 9001 & ISO 14001 Certified Co.,

Regd. Office: 3767A, Kanhaiya Nagar,
Tri Nagar, Delhi-110035
Ph.: 8130886000, 9650072927
E-mail: info@pendownpress.com
Branch Office: 1A/2A, 20, Hari Sadan, Ansari Road,
Daryaganj, New Delhi-110002
Ph.: 011-45794768
Website: PendownPress.com

Edition: 2025
Price: ₹ 399
ISBN: 978-93-6338-273-2

Layout and Cover Designed by Pendown Graphics Team
Printed and Bound in India by Thomson Press India Ltd.

TABLE OF CONTENTS

SPECIAL BONUS CHAPTER

PREFACE

Running a bakery or working in the food business is no cakewalk. It's a blend of art, science, and smart business decisions. Yet, one ingredient often gets overlooked—the oils and fats you use. These unsung heroes quietly decide whether your cake is soft and fluffy or flat and dry. They affect the flavor, texture, and even the shelf life of your products.

Through this book, I want to bring clarity and practical knowledge to help you make smarter choices. Whether you're a baker aiming for consistent taste, a distributor looking for reliable, quality products, or a business owner seeking better margins, this book will be your guide.

You'll discover how the right oils and fats can boost your profits and improve your products without cutting corners. I've also shared real-life experiences and easy-to-apply tips to help you tackle common industry challenges.

- My goal is simple: to empower you with knowledge that helps you grow confidently in a competitive market. So, let's embark on this journey toward better bakes, bigger profits, and happier customers!

ACKNOWLEDGMENTS

Whatever I have achieved in life, would have been impossible without the support of my parents. They've taught me unconditional love and I have seen them grow along with me. The wings that I have today would not have been possible without them.

Dear Dad, It would have been impossible for me to have the vision I do without you. The platform and opportunity I have today are because of you, and I hope I'm able to do justice to them and continue to grow this legacy. You have taught me so many things — most importantly, to be kind, honest, and committed to your work. These family values are deeply imbibed in me, and I strive to pass on these learnings to future generations.

To my wife, who has stood by me in every situation. You have handled all family responsibilities with great skill and dedication. Thank you from the bottom of my heart.

To my children, Aaria and Prithav, who are the source of my happiness and inspiration. Lots of love!

My heartfelt gratitude to all my mentors and guides who have shown me light and direction in times of confusion.

To our clients, who have shared their experiences and knowledge with us during this journey—thank you for trusting us and being our inspiration.

A special acknowledgement goes to Dinesh Verma and his exceptional team at Pendown Press. From the initial concept to the final manuscript, their support and expertise have made this book possible.

And finally, to all my loved ones who have been with me on this journey—thank you for your unwavering support, encouragement, and affection. Even if your names are not mentioned, you always hold a special place in my heart.

Without the support of all of you, it would not have been possible for me to move forward with confidence.

INTRODUCTION

Why This Book?

Running a bakery or food business is not easy. Costs keep going up, customers want better quality, and competition is tough. Many people in this industry follow old methods without knowing the real impact of the oils and fats they use. Some believe that cheaper ingredients will save money, while others think that all oils work the same way. But the truth is, **making the wrong choice can cost you more in the long run.**

This book is written to clear such misunderstandings and help you make smart decisions. You will learn how the right oils and fats can improve the softness and texture of bakery products, increase shelf life, and even make products look bigger without increasing costs. We will also discuss how important the role of consistency in taste is in bringing repeat customers, leading to steady business growth.

Who Is This Book For?

This book is useful for:

1. **Bakery Owners & Bakers:** If you own a bakery or work as a baker, you know that making soft, tasty, and fresh-looking products is the key to attracting customers. This book will teach you how to choose the best oils and fats to improve the softness and texture of your cakes, biscuits, and breads, making them more appealing to buyers.
2. **Distributors & Suppliers**: If you are in the business of selling edible oils, vanaspati, or bakery ingredients, this book will help

you understand what bakers need and how you can provide them with better products. We will also discuss how you can build long-term relationships with your customers and grow your business.

3. **Food Business Owners** – Whether you run a small food outlet shop, a large food manufacturing unit, or a snack company, using the right oils and fats can improve your product quality and increase customer trust. This book will help you make better choices that boost your sales and brand value. (While focusing on bakery fats, even if you don't use them, this book will definitely add value to you and your business).

No matter which category you fall into, if you want to improve product quality, increase customer satisfaction, and grow your business, this book is for you.

My Story - Where It All Began

I was born in 1987, in the heart of **"Dilwalon ki"** Delhi, a city full of energy, culture, and endless stories. I've been fortunate to grow up in a well-cultured joint family environment—one that was rooted in strong values while also embracing an evolving mindset.

My childhood was blissful. Being surrounded by so many family members exposed me to different emotions, situations, and life dynamics that I might not have experienced otherwise.

In my 38 years of life so far, I've been lucky to explore many different industries both through work and personal exposure.

As a child, I was always more curious than playful. While most children my age would get busy playing with their toys or games, I often found myself going deeper into things. It's not that I didn't like toys — in fact, I found them beautiful but what fascinated me more was how they were made. I was more curious about the way it was made, the materials etc than just playing with them.

This way of thinking extended into everything I did — whether it was school, sports, or events. If I was involved in something, I wanted to give it my best. I wasn't just active; I was passionate about being the best at whatever I did. Even during my college days, if I was working on a project, it had to come straight from the heart. This habit helped me succeed in many areas. But whenever my heart wasn't in something, I could feel the difference, the passion just wasn't there.

As I entered the working world, I joined my father's company in 2008. My very first contribution was to make work easier and faster for everyone. I spent over two years relentlessly working to automate many of the processes.

Over time, I got the opportunity to explore various sectors — from hospitality (hotels), textiles, and beverage manufacturing to schools, real estate, steel manufacturing, and of course, the food industry, especially edible oils. For many reasons, I always felt a special connection with the edible oil business. It felt like this is where my heart truly belonged. Through this product, I believed I could reach millions of homes and genuinely make a difference by improving both health and taste.

There's so much potential in the food industry. Even after 15 years, I feel I've only scratched the surface. Being connected to almost every type of food manufacturer in the country exposed me to a wide range of applications and learnings.

With the values imbibed in me, I have always strived to add a positive impact to everyone connected with me, personally or professionally — be it our customers, their customers, team members, vendors, investors, or stakeholders. Adding value to anyone even remotely connected to us is what I live by.

Today, at **Ajanta Soya Ltd.,** we proudly say that anyone in the food industry especially in North India is either our client or closely associated with us. There's a strong chance that many national and regional brands you see and buy every day have **Ajanta's edible oils or specialty fats** as one of their key ingredients.

One of the strongest beliefs I carry — passed on to me by my family and work culture is: **honour your word.** That's how I've always worked, and that's what we stand for.

While oil plays a major role in food, it's also one of the most ignored ingredients. Sadly, it remains one of the most misunderstood categories for the general consumer. Most people don't even know what oil they're using at home. And even those who do, usually know only the brand, not the type or quality of the oil.

- Worse, they may not even know what kind of oil they should be using.

> Oil is often seen as something to be avoided or minimized and in some cases, people even promote oil-free cooking without understanding the science behind it.

Please don't fall into that trap.

Oil is an essential part of the human body. It is important for a healthy life. Yes, it should be consumed in moderation, and no — all oils are not the same.

Even the best oil can be harmful if your lifestyle doesn't support it (for example, if there's no physical activity). On the other hand, even a lower-grade oil may not harm you if combined with the right mix of diet and exercise.

Here's a Quick Activity for You!

Remember those "True or False" sections from our school days? Let's bring that back but this time, with a twist for your business!

Statement	True / False
1. All oils are the same when it comes to baking.	True / False
2. The cheaper the oil, the better it is for your business.	True / False
3. Hydrogenated fats are always harmful, no matter what.	True / False
4. Edible oils don't really affect the softness or shelf life of cakes.	True / False
5. Using different oils for different purposes can improve results.	True / False

Once you go through the next few chapters, come back and check how many you got right.

This topic is vast — so much so that it deserves an entire book on its own. But for now, going deep into oil education is beyond the scope of this book.

With the values imbibed in me, I have always strived to add a positive impact to everyone connected with me, personally or professionally — be it our customers, their customers, team members, vendors, investors, or stakeholders. Adding value to anyone even remotely connected to us is what I live by.

The Evolution of Bakery Oils & Fats

The biggest evolution in the bakery industry was the introduction of specialty fats. Earlier, when these fats were not available, bakers had to source different oils and ghee, mix them in specific proportions, and then further blend them with maida to create the desired batter. This manual mixing process was not only time-consuming but also had its own challenges, particularly in maintaining consistency.

With the advancement of modern technology, the process became significantly more efficient. Today, these oils and ghee are pre-mixed in precise proportions at the factory level, creating ready-to-use bakery fats. This eliminates the need for manual mixing, ensuring consistent quality and saving both time and effort.

Now, every company has its own unique fat mixture recipe, which becomes a signature formula. The company whose mixture perfectly suits the baker's application in the right proportion **WINS** – as it delivers the desired taste, texture, and consistency that customers love.

Oils and fats have always been important in baking, but the way we use them has changed over time. In the past, people used simple ingredients like ghee and butter. Today, we have many options like vanaspati and special bakery fats that make products fluffier, last longer, and look more appealing. For example, fluffiness in cakes and bread makes them look bigger and more attractive, which customers love. At the same time, modern technology using oils and fats help save costs and improve the quality of your products.

However, **finding the perfect balance is not easy.** If an oil makes a product look too dry, customers won't like it. If a fat makes it too sticky, they may not enjoy eating it. The challenge is to select the right combination that gives the best softness and texture without making the product heavy or greasy.

In this book, we will explore how today's bakery businesses, chefs and suppliers can stay ahead in the market by making better choices. With the right knowledge, they can improve the quality of your bakery products while also increasing their profit margins.

CHAPTER 1

THE PROBLEM – CHALLENGES IN THE BAKERY INDUSTRY

"Success is not the key to happiness. Happiness is the key to success. If you love what you are doing, you will be successful." – **Albert Schweitzer**

Running a bakery or food business is not as easy as it looks. Behind the delicious cakes, bread, and snacks, there are many challenges that can make it hard to succeed. In this chapter, we will talk about the biggest problems bakery owners and food manufacturers face every day. These challenges can hurt your profits, frustrate your customers, and make it difficult to grow your business. But don't worry—once you understand these problems, you can start finding solutions.

1. **Struggle for Consistent Taste & Texture - BIGGEST**

   Customers want the same taste every time they buy a product. Whether it's bread, biscuits, or cakes, consistency is key. If one batch of biscuits is crispy and the next batch turns out soft, customers will start doubting the quality. This happens because of differences in ingredients, especially oils and fats.

   Many bakers struggle to maintain the right texture. If the oil is too heavy, products feel greasy. If it's too light, they become dry. Finding the right balance is crucial, but many bakers don't realize that their choice of oil is the main reason behind these variations.

2. **Issues with Low-Quality Oils & Fats**

   The quality of oils and fats you use in your products can make or break your business. Low-quality oils might seem cheaper at first, but they can cause big problems. They can make your products taste bad, spoil faster, or even harm your customers' health. For example, some oils leave a sticky feeling in the mouth, which customers don't like. Others might not give your products the fluffiness or softness they need. Using poor-quality oils might save you money in the short term, but in the long run, it can cost you customers and profits.

3. **Demand Fluctuations & Distribution Inefficiencies**

   Another big challenge is dealing with changes in customer demand. Some days, you might sell out of everything, while on other days, you're left with unsold products. This can lead to waste and lost money. At the same time, getting the right ingredients on time can be a headache. If your distributor is late or doesn't deliver the right quantity, it can disrupt your entire production. These inefficiencies in distribution and demand planning can make it hard to run your business smoothly.

4. **The Hidden Cost of Poor-Quality Ingredients**

   Many bakery owners think that using cheaper ingredients will help them save money. But this is often a big mistake. Poor-quality ingredients might cost less upfront, but they can lead to hidden costs. For example, if your products don't taste good or spoil quickly, customers will stop buying them. You might also waste time and money fixing problems caused by bad ingredients. In the end, using low-quality oils and fats can actually cost you more than using good ones.

5. **Increased Competition & Shrinking Margins**

   The bakery industry is becoming more competitive every day. New bakeries are opening, and big companies are offering cheaper products. At the same time, the cost of ingredients, labor, and rent is going up. This means your profit margins are getting smaller. To survive in this tough market, you need to find ways to stand out. Whether it's by improving the quality of your products, reducing costs, or offering something unique, you need a plan to stay ahead of the competition.

These challenges might seem overwhelming, but they are not impossible to solve. The first step is to understand what's causing these problems in your business. Once you know the root cause, you can start looking for solutions.

Remember, every problem has a solution—you just need to know where to look.

REFLECTION ACTIVITY

What's Holding You Back?

Take a few minutes to reflect on the challenges you face in your own bakery or food business.

☑ What's relevant? Tick it:

- ☐ I struggle to maintain consistent taste and texture in my products.
- ☐ I often use lower-cost oils without knowing their quality or effect.
- ☐ My distributor is unreliable or causes delays.
- ☐ I face demand fluctuations and often deal with leftover or wasted stock.

Question:

Which one challenge above is hurting your business the most right now?

____

____

____

____

CHAPTER 2

MYTHS ABOUT BAKERY OILS & FATS

"The only way to do great work is to love what you do."
– Steve Jobs

In the bakery business, there are many myths and misconceptions about oils and fats. These myths can lead to poor decisions, wasted money, and unhappy customers. In this chapter, we will bust some of the most common myths and explain why they are not true. By understanding the facts, you can make better choices for your business and create products that your customers will love.

Myth #1: All Oils Work the Same Way

Some people think that oil is just oil—meaning any type can be used in any recipe. But that's far from true. Different oils and fats react differently during baking and frying.

- **Palm-based fats** are great for crispy biscuits.
- **Vanaspati** provides richness but should be balanced correctly.
- **Butter & ghee** add flavor but don't provide the same structure as specialty fats.
- **Liquid oils** work in some cakes but don't provide the same

fluffiness as solid fats.

- **Manufacturer's Composition:** This is by far the most underrated factor that affects the end product of a bakery.
- **Location of Manufacturing Unit vs. Bakery:** Temperature greatly affects the texture of fats used. A difference in the temperature of the manufacturing location versus the user location, or even a time gap as small as 15 days between manufacturing and usage (especially during changing seasons), can significantly affect the end product experience for bakery customers.

Using the wrong oil can result in dry, hard, or soggy products, ruining customer experience. Choosing the right fat is essential for maintaining product quality.

Myth #2: Vanaspati is Outdated and Unhealthy

Many people believe that vanaspati is unhealthy and outdated in modern baking. However, this is not entirely true. Vanaspati still plays a significant role in bakery products and is not disappearing anytime soon. Interestingly, in countries where vanaspati was never a traditional product, the demand for hydrogenated vegetable oils is still growing. For example, the United States, Canada, and several European nations have used hydrogenated vegetable oils in baking and food processing for decades. This shows that even Western food industries continue to rely on such oils, despite the ongoing health debates.

- **Improves texture:** It helps in giving better softness and mouthfeel.
- **More refined than before:** Modern vanaspati has lower trans fats, making it a better choice than before.
- **Cost-effective:** When used in the right proportion, it helps

small bakeries maintain consistent quality without increasing costs.

The key is not to overuse it. When combined with other fats in the right ratio, vanaspati can enhance product quality while keeping costs under control.

Myth #3: More Ghee Means Better Quality

Ghee is often seen as the ultimate premium ingredient, but using more ghee doesn't always mean a better product.

Here's why:

- **Strong flavor:** Ghee has a distinct taste that can overpower the actual flavor of baked products.
- **Expensive:** It significantly increases production costs without necessarily improving texture or shelf life.
- **Not ideal for all products:** While ghee adds richness and flavor, it lacks the structural properties needed in certain recipes.

  For example:

  - Cakes and pastries may turn dense due to ghee's low moisture.
  - Cookies can become drier and brittle.
  - Bread may lose elasticity, affecting texture.

Thus, while ghee enhances flavor, it isn't always the best fit for every baked product. That's why it is not ideal for all.

Instead of blindly using more ghee, bakers should focus on balancing different fats to achieve the best texture, taste, and cost-efficiency.

Myth #4: Specialty Fats Are Only for Large-Scale Production

Many small and medium-sized bakers assume that specialty fats are meant only for big factories with massive output. The common belief is, **"We're too small to need such advanced ingredients."**

But this mindset often holds growing businesses back.

Here's the truth: **Specialty fats are not about the size of your production—they're about the quality and consistency of your products.** In fact, small and mid-sized bakeries can benefit even more from them because every single batch and every repeat customer matters.

Here's how specialty fats actually help *businesses of all sizes:*

- **Consistency, Batch after Batch**: Whether you bake 50 cakes or 5000, specialty fats help maintain the same softness, structure, and taste every time — no surprises.
- **Longer shelf life**: Products stay fresher for longer, which is especially important if your sales are spread over a few days. It means fewer returns, fewer stale items, and happier customers.
- **Improved volume & texture**: Some specialty fats are designed for better aeration and structure, giving your cakes, puffs, or cookies that "wow" factor — light, fluffy, and picture-perfect.
- **Cost savings in the long run**: While specialty fats may cost more per kg upfront, they reduce production errors, wastage, and customer complaints—saving money and building loyalty over time.

Smart bakers invest in better ingredients because they know that quality = customer satisfaction = repeat sales.

Myth #5: Oil Doesn't Affect Volume & Fluffiness

Many bakers think that only flour and yeast determine how fluffy a product will be. But oils and fats play a crucial role in volume and texture.

- **Right oils help in air incorporation,** making the product light and airy.
- **Some oils create a dense dough,** reducing fluffiness.
- **Poor oil choices cause excess greasiness,** ruining the final texture.

For example, a cake made with the wrong oil might rise beautifully in the oven but collapse after cooling because the structure was weak. Using the right fat ensures the perfect balance between softness and stability.

Myth #6: Chef Change with Same Ingredients Won't Affect Customer Experience

Many people believe that if they use the same ingredients, the end product will always be the same, no matter who prepares it. This is not true. The skill and experience of the chef play a big role in the final product. For example, two chefs can use the same recipe and ingredients, but one might make a cake that's soft and fluffy, while the other might end up with a dense and dry cake. The process—how the ingredients are mixed, baked, and handled—matters just as much as the ingredients themselves. Consistency in process is key to delivering the same great experience to your customers every time.

Myth #7: Role of Availability in Consistency

Some bakers believe that ingredient availability doesn't impact their product quality much. They think switching brands temporarily won't make a difference. But in reality, inconsistent ingredient sourcing causes major issues.

- **Different melting points**: Oils and fats from different brands have **slightly different properties**, affecting texture and mouthfeel.
- **Flavor variations**: Even if two fats have the same label, their flavor profiles may differ slightly, creating inconsistencies in taste.
- **Unreliable supply = inconsistent product:** When bakers frequently switch between suppliers due to availability issues, the end product keeps changing, frustrating loyal customers.

To maintain consistent quality, bakers need to secure a reliable supply chain with trusted vendors.

REFLECTION ACTIVITY

What's Holding You Back?

Take a few minutes to reflect on the challenges you face in your own bakery or food business.

What's relevant? Tick it:

- [ ] I choose oils based mainly on price, not on quality or performance.
- [ ] My supplier is often inconsistent or fails to deliver on time.
- [ ] I end up with unsold stock due to unpredictable demand.
- [ ] I feel constant pressure from new or cheaper competitors.

Question:

Which one challenge above is hurting your business the most right now?

____

____

____

____

CHAPTER 3

THE LEGACY OF PREMIUM BAKERY FATS

"Whatever you do, do it so well that people will want to see it again and bring others to see it too."
- Walt Disney

When it comes to running a successful bakery, the quality of your ingredients can make all the difference. Among these ingredients, bakery fats and oils play a starring role. Premium bakery fats are not just about making your products taste better—they are about building trust, ensuring consistency, and increasing profitability. In this chapter, we'll explore why premium bakery fats are worth the investment and how they can help you create a legacy of quality and success.

1. **Building Trust Through Quality**

   Customers don't just buy your products—they buy the trust they have in your brand. When you use premium bakery fats, you're sending a clear message that you care about quality. For example, a cake made with high-quality fats will have a better texture, richer flavor, and longer shelf life. Customers will notice the difference and keep coming back for more. Over time, this builds a loyal customer base that trusts your brand. Whether you're a small bakery or a large food manufacturer, trust is the foundation of long-term success.

2. **The Role of Legacy Brands**

Legacy brands in the bakery and food industry didn't become successful overnight. Their reputation was built over years of delivering consistent quality and one key to that consistency lies in their choice of ingredients, especially premium bakery fats. These brands understand that quality isn't just about the final taste; it starts with what goes into the product.

By choosing premium fats, you're not just improving your recipes—you're following a proven path that successful brands have walked for decades. It's about creating a lasting impression. When customers remember the taste, softness, and freshness of your products, they remember **you**. That's how legacies are built.

For most bakery owners, the journey starts with a deep love for good food—a passion for taste, creativity, and the dream of building something meaningful. But soon, practical realities set in. Bills need to be paid. Margins matter. And it's tempting to compromise by choosing cheaper ingredients.

But here's the truth: cheaper ingredients might save a little in the short run, but they often attract price-sensitive customers who hop from one shop to another for minor discounts. These customers rarely become loyal buyers—and they rarely help you grow.

Instead, consider this balanced approach: continue your regular business operations, but at the same time, **develop a separate line of high-quality products** using premium fats. These can be targeted at customers who value quality and are willing to pay more for it.

Over time, this second line can become your most profitable one. It builds a reputation, attracts loyal customers, and sets you apart from the competition.

And who knows? That shift toward quality might bring in higher profits – **sooner than you think.**

3. How Premium Oils Increase Profitability

At first glance, premium bakery fats might seem more expensive than regular ones. But in reality, they can actually help you save money and increase profits. Here's how:

- **Better Shelf Life = Less Waste**: Premium fats extend the freshness of your products by several days. For example, if your regular cakes stay fresh for 3 days, using better fats might increase that to 5-7 days.

  Result: Less wastage, fewer unsold returns, and more chances to sell the same product.

- **Consistent Quality = Repeat Customers:** Let's say 2 out of 5 customers don't come back because of taste or texture differences. That's a 40% loss in repeat sales. With consistent quality, you reduce that risk and build stronger customer retention.

- **Higher Margins = Better Profit:** Premium-quality products command a higher selling price.

  Example: Regular Cake vs. Premium Cake

  Let's say you sell a regular cake for ₹500, and the cost to make it using regular fats is ₹350. Profit = ₹150.

  Now, you decide to improve the quality by using premium fats, which increases your cost slightly to ₹375. But because of the better texture, softness, and shelf life, you can confidently price it at ₹600. **Profit = ₹225.**

That's **₹75 more profit per cake**, a **50% increase in profit**—all because of a small shift in ingredients and a better value proposition to your customer.

And guess what?

Customers are usually happy to pay more when they can see and taste the difference. You don't just earn more—you build loyalty and word-of-mouth.

- **Fewer Errors = More Efficient Production:** Premium fats perform more consistently during baking. You'll notice better spread, puffiness, and moisture, with fewer batches wasted due to inconsistency.

  This saves both time and money on rework or spoilage.

- **Loyal Customers:** Price-sensitive buyers may come and go—but quality-focused customers stay longer. Loyal customers tend to buy more frequently, recommend you to others, and are less likely to switch.

A Quick Comparison

Category	Regular Fats	Premium Fats
Cost per kg	₹100	₹130
Shelf Life	3 days	6–7 days
Product Returns	Higher	Lower
Selling Price Range	₹25–₹30	₹35–₹40
Customer Loyalty	Low	High
Long-Term Profitability	Low	High

Bottom Line

Investing in premium fats is not an extra cost—it's a smart strategy. You improve quality, build customer loyalty, reduce wastage, and open doors to higher pricing.

Would you rather save ₹5 per kg today or earn ₹20 more per product tomorrow?

4. **The Science Behind Perfect Baking Fats**

   What makes premium bakery fats so special? It's all about science. Premium fats are designed to perform specific functions that improve your products:

   - **Fluffiness and Volume:** Some fats are engineered to trap air, making cakes and pastries lighter and fluffier.
   - **Moisture Retention:** Premium fats help retain moisture, keeping your products soft and fresh for longer.
   - **Stability:** They are more stable at high temperatures, ensuring consistent results during baking.
   - **Flavor Enhancement:** High-quality fats enhance the natural flavors of your ingredients, making your products taste better.

Understanding the science behind these fats can help you choose the right ones for your recipes and achieve the perfect results every time.

Why Premium Bakery Fats Matter

Premium bakery fats aren't just ingredients—they're game-changers for your business. They elevate the quality of your products, helping you stand out in a competitive market. With better texture, flavor, and consistency, you'll build customer trust and loyalty. Plus, premium fats can boost your profitability by allowing you to charge higher prices for superior products.

While the focus here is on bakeries, the benefits of using high-quality fats apply to any food business looking for exceptional taste and consistency.

5. **Role of Fats and Oils in Frying, Baking and Confectionery Applications**

   Frying food is an important part of the human food chain and is done for multiple reasons, including enhancing taste. Additionally, frying increases the shelf life of the product due to several factors.

   Deep frying is typically done at approximately 180°C, a temperature at which moisture in the food is completely evaporated. Most bacteria and live viruses are either killed or rendered inactive at this temperature. Moreover, the dissolved or attached oxygen in the food is expelled during frying, creating an environment that is unfavorable for the growth of microorganisms, including fungi. During frying, proteins coagulate, which also acts as a taste enhancer. All these factors combined help the product resist oxidative rancidity, thereby increasing its shelf life.

   It is worth mentioning that specific oils are preferred for particular frying applications. For example, pungent mustard oil is favored for frying aquatic creatures like fish, prawns, and crabs, as it enhances their natural flavor and aroma. On the other hand, cottonseed oil and palmolein are commonly used for snacks like bhujia, namkeen mixtures, chips, and fryums due to their neutral taste and cost-effectiveness. From a health perspective, nutrition experts have proposed various blends to improve frying oils.

Modern technology has enabled the conversion of oils into fats through processes like hydrogenation and inter-esterification. These fats serve as cooking media that are more thermally stable and resistant to oxidation, making them particularly suitable for deep frying, including repeated frying.

Another important food preservation technique is baking, which also requires oils or fats for specific applications, especially to resist oxidative rancidity. Apart from enhancing taste, fats contribute to the desired texture, fluffiness, and shine in products such as biscuits, kharis, and other puffy eatables. In these applications, solidified fats with smooth textures are preferred over liquid oils because soft oils tend to ooze out before baking is complete, defeating their purpose. These specialized fats are known as specialty fats. The blends and techniques used in making these fats for specific applications require the expertise of skilled fat makers.

The third and most important application of specialty fats is found in products like chocolates and ice creams, where fat is the key component. Here, fat influences the "mouthfeel," meaning the product melts and spreads smoothly and uniformly on the tongue, creating a complete and pleasant sensory experience for the consumer.

Wrapping It All Together: Quality Is the Quiet Hero

From fluffy cakes to crispy fryums and melt-in-your-mouth chocolates, premium bakery fats play a silent but powerful role in every bite your customers enjoy. They are not just technical ingredients—they are the backbone of consistency, shelf life, taste, and customer loyalty.

In a competitive market where every product fights for attention, quality becomes your edge. And premium fats are your partners in creating that quality—batch after batch, customer after customer.

Think of them not just as an added cost, but as an investment into your brand's future—a step toward creating a reputation that people remember, return to, and recommend.

REFLECTION ACTIVITY

What's Holding You Back?

Take a few minutes to reflect on the challenges you face in your own bakery or food business.

☑ What's relevant? Tick it:

- ☐ My profits look fine, but I don't feel I'm building a strong, lasting brand.
- ☐ I've compromised on ingredient quality just to manage monthly expenses.
- ☐ I rely on price to attract customers instead of standing out for quality.
- ☐ I worry that my products aren't consistent enough to earn customer loyalty.

Question:

What's one small step you can take this week/month to start building a reputation for quality?

____

____

____

____

CHAPTER 4

THE FUTURE OF BAKERY OILS & FATS

"If you can't do great things, do small things in a great way." - **Napoleon Hill**

The bakery industry is evolving fast, and so are the oils and fats used in baking. With changing consumer preferences, health trends, and technological advancements, bakery oils and fats are no longer just about taste and texture. They are now about health, sustainability, and efficiency. In this chapter, we'll talk about the latest trends and how you can use them to grow your bakery business.

1. Emerging Trends in Bakery Oils & Fats

The bakery industry is witnessing a shift towards premium, specialized fats that offer more than just richness. Some of the major trends include:

- **Functional oils**: These oils are enriched with Omega-3, vitamins, or antioxidants, adding nutritional value to baked products.
- **Customized fat blends**: Many bakeries are switching to tailor-made fat combinations that offer better volume, stability, and texture consistency.

- **Low-to-zero trans-fat and clean-label oils**: With growing health awareness, the demand for clean-label oils (free from artificial additives) is on the rise.
- **The fluffiness trade-off: taste vs. health:** High-trans oils offer better fluffiness and texture in baked and fried foods but come with serious health risks. In contrast, zero-trans oils are healthier but result in less fluffiness. Gradually shifting to healthier blends and innovative techniques can help balance quality and wellness.

Example: Many premium bakeries now use butter-oil blends to get the richness of butter while maintaining the cost-effectiveness of oil.

2. **Health-Conscious and Low-Trans-Fat Innovations**

Health is a top priority for today's customers, and they are looking for bakery products that fit their lifestyle. This has led to the rise of low-trans-fat and zero-trans-fat oils and fats. These healthier options not only meet customer demands but also comply with stricter food regulations.

This is pushing the bakery industry towards:

- **Low-trans-fat and cholesterol-free oils**: Healthier fats help bakeries cater to the **health-focused audience**, making their products more marketable.
- **Plant-based fats**: With the rise of vegan and vegetarian lifestyles, plant-based oils and fat alternatives are gaining popularity. Since most bakery fats in the general market are already plant-based (mainly palm fruit-based fats), the trend is shifting towards more sustainable and non-GMO plant fat sources.
- **Reduced saturated fats**: More bakers are opting for high-

performance oils with lower saturated fats while still delivering the same fluffiness and mouthfeel. However, this comes with a **trade-off** between health benefits and the product's texture, stability, and shelf life.

Fact: MR and Allied Market Research which showed that "The margarine market was valued at $22.1 billion in 2023, and is estimated to reach $29.2 billion by 2033, growing at a CAGR of 2.9% from 2024 to 2033.

3. **Sustainable Sourcing & Eco-Friendly Production**

   The future of bakery oils isn't just about quality—it's also about sustainability. More brands are moving towards:

   - **Sustainably sourced palm oil:** Many companies now use RSPO-certified palm oil, ensuring it comes from sustainable plantations, or have started enquiring and have a clear plan to switch in the next few years.
   - **Eco-friendly production**: Bakery oil manufacturers are reducing waste, optimizing energy usage, and minimizing water consumption during production.
   - **Recyclable packaging**: More brands are investing in biodegradable and recyclable packaging, reducing their environmental footprint. This has become standard.

Eco Tip: Using sustainably sourced fats not only improves your bakery's reputation but also appeals to eco-conscious customers.

4. **How AI & Technology Are Changing Bakery Oil Manufacturing**

   Technology is playing a big role in enhancing the quality and consistency of bakery oils and fats. With the help of AI and automation:

- **Precise blending and refining:** Automated systems, including PLC-based controls, ensure accurate blending of fats and oils, delivering consistent, high-quality batches.
- **Quality control and testing**: Automated systems scan for impurities and inconsistencies, improving overall product safety and quality.
- **Smart supply chain management**: AI is helping manufacturers predict demand, ensuring bakeries always have a consistent supply of quality fats.

Example: Some oil manufacturers use AI-driven quality checks to maintain the perfect melting point for bakery fats, ensuring consistent baking performance.

5. **Predicting the Next Decade: What's Next for Bakery Oils?**

The future of bakery oils and fats is poised for exciting changes, driven by innovation, consumer preferences, and sustainability. Here's what you can expect in the coming decade:

- **Personalized Nutrition:** As diets like keto and gluten-free continue to grow in popularity, bakery oils and fats will evolve to meet these specific needs. Expect oils formulated to support dietary trends, with a focus on health benefits like reduced saturated fats and enhanced omega-3 content.
- **Clean Label Products:** Consumers are increasingly seeking products with simple, transparent ingredient lists. This trend will push bakery oil manufacturers to offer oils made from natural, recognizable ingredients, without artificial additives or preservatives, providing a healthier and more authentic experience for customers.
- **Innovative Flavors:** To stay competitive, bakery oils will begin offering unique flavors and textures that elevate

bakery products. Think oils infused with herbs, spices, or even fruit essences, bringing exciting new taste profiles to everything from pastries to bread.

- **Circular Economy:** As sustainability becomes a priority, the bakery oil industry will focus on reducing waste. This could include new methods of recycling oil byproducts or innovations in packaging that are more eco-friendly, supporting a circular economy and reducing environmental impact.

In summary, the next decade will be marked by oils that are not only healthier and more sustainable but also tailored to the individual tastes and needs of consumers. By keeping an eye on these developments, you'll be able to adapt, innovate, and future-proof your bakery for continued success.

REFLECTION ACTIVITY

What's Holding You Back?

Take a few minutes to reflect on the challenges you face in your own bakery or food business.

☑ What's relevant? Tick it:

- ☐ I've not yet explored low-trans-fat or clean-label options for my products.
- ☐ I still rely on traditional fats without considering newer, healthier alternatives.
- ☐ I rarely think about how my oil choices impact my product's health perception.
- ☐ I feel confused by the tech and trend changes in bakery fats and oils.

Question:

If you could adopt just one trend (like clean-label, AI-driven supply, or plant-based fats), which one feels most aligned with your brand's future and why?

____

____

____

____

CHAPTER 5

CHOOSING THE RIGHT BAKERY OILS & FATS FOR YOUR BUSINESS

"Excellence is not an act, but a habit." - **Aristotle**

Choosing the right oils and fats for your bakery is one of the most important decisions you'll make. The oils you use affect the taste, texture, and quality of your products and ultimately, your profits. In this chapter, we'll help you understand the different types of bakery fats and oils, how to pick the best ones, and how to balance cost and quality. Let's get started!

1. **Understanding Different Types of Bakery Fats & Oils**

   Not all oils and fats are the same. Each type has its own unique properties, and choosing the right one depends on what you're baking. Here are some common types:

Types of Bakery Fats & Oils

Type	Specialty / Key Feature	Best Used For
Refined Oils	Neutral taste, light, and versatile	Cakes, cookies, bread

Vanaspati	Rich texture, affordable, all-purpose fat	Bread, pastries, biscuits
Bakery Shortenings	Provides fluffiness, volume, and aeration	Cakes, pastries, cream fillings
Ghee	Traditional flavor, aromatic, heavy if overused	Indian-style bakery products, festive items
Butter	Rich flavor, soft texture, premium feel	Premium cookies, cakes, croissants
Palm Oil & Blends	Long shelf life, stable at room temp, consistent results	Mass-produced cakes, cookies, breads
Margarine	Cost-effective butter alternative, fluffy and stable texture	Pastries, cookies, laminated doughs

Understanding these options will help you pick the right fat or oil for each recipe.

2. **The Role of Fats in Creating Puffiness and Texture**

   Choosing the right fat is not just about flavor or cost—it plays a critical role in the texture and structure of bakery products. For items like puff pastry, croissants, and biscuits, the fat's ability to create flaky, airy layers through puffing is essential. Let's explore how puffing works and why fat selection is crucial in this process.

   Puffing in bakery products, particularly puff pastry, is achieved through a process called laminated dough, where layers of fat and dough are repeatedly folded and rolled. This creates a flaky, airy texture when baked, as steam from the water in the dough expands and puffs up the layers.

Essentially, puffing occurs through the repeated folding and rolling of alternating layers of dough and fat, followed by resting the dough in a refrigerator or other cold space. This resting period helps the gluten relax and allows the fat to solidify, preventing it from melting too quickly during baking.

Want to see the real technique behind creating perfect puffiness?

Scan the QR Code below to watch our step-by-step folding method in a real recipe demonstration:

3. **How to Identify High-Quality Oils for Baking**

High-quality oils and fats can make a big difference in your bakery products. Here's how to spot them:

- **Check the Label**: Look for oils with simple, natural ingredients and no harmful additives.
- **Test the Performance**: Good oils should give your products a consistent texture, taste, and shelf life.
- **Ask for Certifications:** Look for industry-standard certifications such as:
    - **FSSAI (Food Safety and Standards Authority of India):** Mandatory for all food products in India. It ensures basic hygiene and safety compliance.

    - **AGMARK:** Government certification for agricultural products including oils, indicating purity and quality.
    - **ISI Mark (from BIS - Bureau of Indian Standards):** Optional, but adds credibility to the oil's manufacturing standards.
    - **GMP Certification (Good Manufacturing Practices):** Shows that the oil is produced under safe and standardized conditions.
- **Read Reviews:** See what other bakers are saying about the oil or fat you're considering.
- **Location of Manufacturer:** Fresher produce is more suitable for local temperature changes (those who understand this better). New manufacturers enter the business hoping to replicate what years of experience have taught them.

By choosing high-quality oils, you can create better products and keep your customers happy.

4. **Cost vs. Quality: Finding the Right Balance**

   It's tempting to go for cheaper oils to save money, but this can cost you more in the long run. Low-quality oils can ruin the taste and texture of your products, leading to unhappy customers and wasted ingredients. On the other hand, premium oils might cost more upfront, but they can help you:

   - **Don't compromise on core products:** For your signature items (cakes, puffs, or cookies), always use premium oils to maintain consistent quality.
   - **Use economical fats strategically:** For low-cost or bulk products, use cost-efficient blends without sacrificing too much on quality.

- **Monitor oil wastage:** Train your staff to use oils efficiently, avoiding overuse or spillage, which can inflate your costs unnecessarily.

The key is to find a balance between cost and quality that works for your business.

REFLECTION ACTIVITY

What's Holding You Back?

Take a few minutes to reflect on the challenges you face in your own bakery or food business.

☑ What's relevant? Tick it:

- ☐ I choose fats based on price first, even if I'm unsure about their performance.
- ☐ I've never fully understood the difference between shortening, margarine, and vanaspati—I just go by what my supplier says.
- ☐ I don't regularly train my staff on how to store or use oils and fats properly.
- ☐ I've never compared the shelf life of my products using different fat options.

Question:

If you had to pick one product in your bakery to upgrade with a better-quality fat or oil, which one would it be and why?

____

____

____

____

CHAPTER 6

MAXIMIZING PROFITABILITY WITH SMART OIL & FAT USAGE

"Arise, awake, and stop not till the goal is reached."
– Swami Vivekananda

Running a profitable bakery isn't just about selling more products—it's also about using your ingredients wisely. When it comes to oils and fats, smart management can cut costs, reduce waste, and improve product quality, all of which directly impact your bottom line. By making a few strategic changes, you can increase your profits without sacrificing quality. Let's explore how you can do it effectively.

1. **Reducing Waste and Pilferage in Distribution**

   In many bakeries, small amounts of oil or fat are wasted every day during distribution. Whether it's due to over-pouring, spillage, or pilferage, these minor losses add up over time and reduce your profit margins.

   What You Can Do:

   Use Pre-Measured Dispensers

   Pouring oils directly from large cans often leads to overuse.

A better approach is to switch to pre-measured dispensers, pumps, or sachets. These tools help you control the exact amount of oil or fat used per batch, ensuring consistency in recipes and minimizing waste.

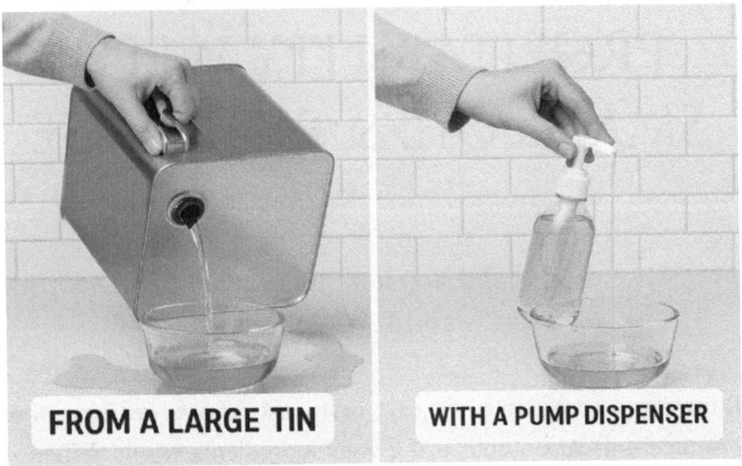

Reduce Pilferage with Simple Systems

Oil pilferage is a hidden cost that often goes unnoticed—small amounts taken frequently can add up to major losses.

You should:

- Maintain a daily usage log for oils and fats.
- Store oils in locked cabinets or monitored areas.
- Assign access to only responsible kitchen or store staff.

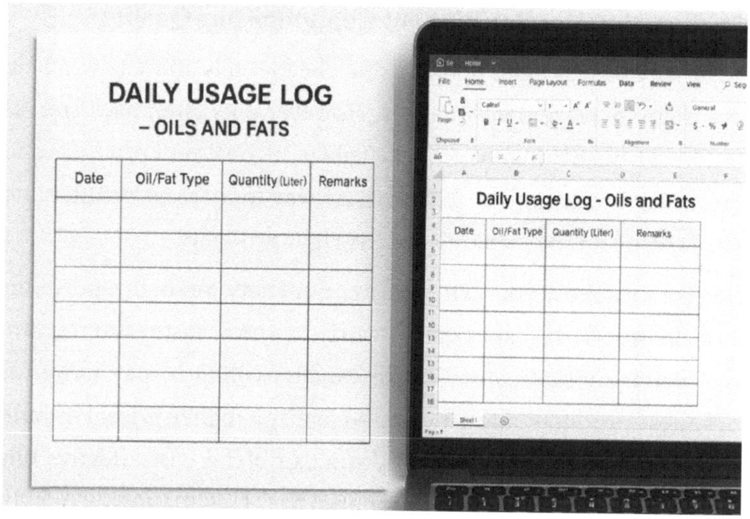

Track & Save

Even a basic stock-tracking system (manual or digital) can help you notice patterns, spot sudden spikes in usage, and take corrective action. Over time, this leads to lower wastage, better accountability, and higher profits.

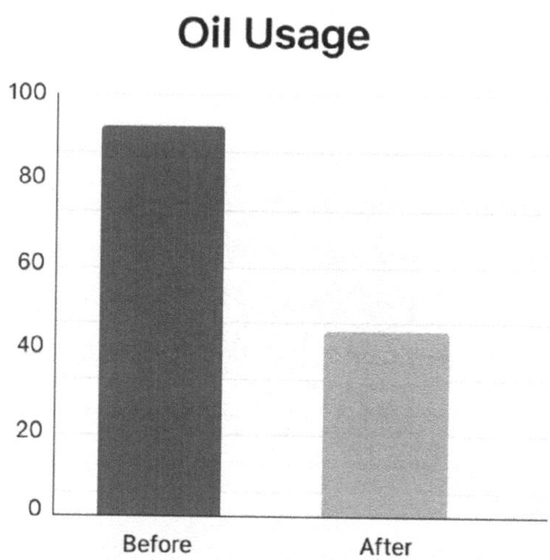

2. **Boosting Margins Without Compromising Quality**

   Many bakers assume that using cheaper oils and fats will help them increase their margins. However, this often backfires, as lower-quality ingredients can lead to inconsistent products and unhappy customers. The smarter way to increase profitability is by using the right oils for the right products.

   For instance, you can use premium fats for high-end items like specialty cakes and pastries, where taste and texture matter most. Customers are usually willing to pay more for these products, allowing you to justify a higher price. For bulk items like bread or biscuits, you can blend cost-effective oils with a small amount of premium fat. This maintains quality while keeping production costs low, giving you a better profit margin.

   Additionally, improving your recipes with the right oil combinations can enhance the flavor and texture of your products, allowing you to market them as premium offerings. This creates an opportunity to charge slightly more without increasing costs significantly.

Please scan this QR code to sign up and get access to our full set of bakery recipes.

3. **Storing Oils & Fats Properly to Avoid Spoilage**

   One major issue in bakeries is that oils and fats can go bad if not stored properly. When oils become rancid, they not only affect taste but can also cause health issues. Spoiled ingredients lead to waste, which directly impacts profits.

   To prevent this, store oils in a cool, dark place, away from direct sunlight and heat. Keeping them in sealed containers reduces exposure to air, which slows down spoilage. Also, always follow the FIFO (First In, First Out) method—use the older stock first so nothing goes to waste.

   By following proper storage practices, you can use your oils and fats over a longer period without quality loss. This reduces spoilage, lowers ingredient waste, and improves your overall profitability.

REFLECTION ACTIVITY

What's Holding You Back?

Take a few minutes to reflect on the challenges you face in your own bakery or food business.

☑ What's relevant? Tick it:

- ☐ I've noticed oil or fat going to waste due to over-pouring or careless handling.
- ☐ I still use large tins or jars, even though I know measured dispensing might help.
- ☐ I don't have a system in place to track daily oil/fat usage or stock movement.
- ☐ Some of my products don't justify the cost of the premium fats I'm using.

Question:

What's one small change you can make this week to reduce waste or improve profit margins?

____

____

____

____

CHAPTER 7

SUCCESS STORIES – BAKERS & DISTRIBUTORS WHO GOT IT RIGHT

"Great things are not done by impulse, but by a series of small things brought together."
– Vincent Van Gogh

1. Case Study of Mr. Birendra Nath Sharma

My name is Birendra Nath Sharma, and I'm the proprietor of Nath & Son. I started the trading business in 2004 along with my father, who had served as a Captain in the Army. After his retirement, we decided to begin a new chapter together—our own business. With no prior background in trade and only a small room in our home to work from, our journey began with more courage than capital.

In the early days, lack of funds and experience posed significant challenges. To introduce ghee in bakeries, we would often spend nights at the production sites conducting trials. At that time, bakery shortening was not commonly used. Most bakers depended on granular vanaspati ghee, which had to be melted and cooled before it could be used—a hectic and time-consuming process.

Over time, we encouraged the shift toward bakery shortening, educating customers about its efficiency and benefits. **Around 2009, we transitioned to using Ajanta's products and that decision brought a noticeable difference.** The consistency, quality, and reliability of their materials gave us the confidence to scale. What stood out most was the stability in product performance, which helped us build trust with our own customers.

Today, around 3,000 tons of bakery fat are sold monthly in Delhi, and I'm proud to say that Nath & Son contributes nearly 800 tons to that figure of which a major share comes from Ajanta's offerings.

The journey hasn't been easy. We still encounter several hurdles:

1. **Cash Management**: The industry largely runs on small-denomination cash transactions, making direct bank deposits difficult. This requires us to convert the cash into higher denominations, incurring extra costs.
2. **Delayed Payments**: On average, payments are delayed by two to three months, creating cash flow issues.
3. **High-Risk Transactions**: Operating in a small-scale industry means bearing the risk of unpaid dues. We face yearly losses of ₹10 to ₹20 lakh due to delayed or defaulted payments.

Yet, we remain committed to growth. We consistently work on introducing new products and adapting to market needs. Much of our progress is due to long-standing support from trusted partners like Ajanta, and our dedication to maintaining consistency in taste and quality.

Looking ahead, our target is to scale our sales to 1,500 tons monthly. With continued innovation, resilience, and strong partnerships, we believe the road ahead is promising. And with Ajanta by our side, offering consistent quality and dependable support—we're confident that this milestone is well within reach.

"न था कोई अनुभव, न थी कोई पहचान,
बस थी लगन और सपनों का जहान।
अजन्ता ने जब दिया भरोसे का साथ,
तब बिखरी अंधेरों में रौशनी की बात।"

– बीरेंद्र नाथ शर्मा

2. Case Study of Mr. Ishan Jain, CEO Achrumal & Sons

We are proud to introduce Achrumal & Sons as a legacy-driven enterprise, with a rich history spanning over three decades since its inception in 1994. Our foray into the bakery fats industry began with ABC Company (Amrit Vanaspati), and over the years, we have had the opportunity to collaborate with several leading names in the industry.

Like many enduring businesses, our journey has not been without challenges. From navigating the complexities of new product launches and payment recoveries—often involving extended credit cycles—to adapting to shifting company policies and facing occasional financial setbacks, we've experienced it all. However, our true turning point came when we partnered with Ajanta Soya Limited.

This partnership marked a new chapter of growth and stability. Ajanta entrusted us with key markets across Delhi, Western Uttar Pradesh, and Punjab, supporting us consistently across multiple fronts—competitive pricing, consistent product quality, reliable deliveries, credit flexibility, and marketing initiatives. The association became even more synergistic with the onboarding of Mr. Sanjay Sharma, whose leadership and vision have been instrumental in our continued success.

We are especially grateful to the leadership and promoters of Ajanta Soya for their steadfast support and belief in our capabilities. Today, Achrumal & Sons handles a monthly volume of approximately 1,200–1,500 tons in the bakery segment, and we look forward to scaling even greater heights in partnership with Ajanta Soya in the years to come.

"हर मुश्किल राह में अजन्ता
बना था भरोसे का नाम,
उसी संग बढ़े क़दम और पाया
हमने व्यापार में नया मुकाम।"

– ईशान जैन

3. Case Study of Mr. Manmohan Sharma

In 1990, I, Manmohan Sharma, founded Salty Food Products under the brand name Mohan's in a modest 600-square-yard space. Starting on my own, I began by producing and selling namkeen directly in the market. Breaking into an already established market was challenging—shopkeepers were hesitant to give shelf space to an unknown brand. Despite limited resources and recognition, we persevered, focusing on building our reputation through consistent quality.

We continuously conducted market research and introduced new products to meet evolving consumer demands. I personally handled every aspect of the business—from driving the delivery van to managing sales and accounting. In those early days, competition was less intense than it is today. Our focus on delivering high-quality namkeen gradually earned us customer trust. As demand grew, we transitioned from direct sales to a distribution model, expanding our reach and building a team of sales and finance professionals.

By 2000, increasing demand for variety prompted us to set up our own bakery production unit. Until then, we had relied on external manufacturers for biscuits, which limited our control over quality. Drawing from a decade of experience, we realized that taste and quality are the cornerstones of success in the food industry. We invested in a bhatti (oven) and built a skilled team to produce biscuits in-house, exactly to our specifications. This decision significantly improved our product quality and market response.

We never compromised on raw materials, consistently using the finest maida (refined flour), ghee (clarified butter), refined oil, spices, and high-grade packaging. Our unwavering commitment to quality became the foundation of our growing sales.

One key factor that supported this growth was our decision to work with Ajanta. While we had earlier faced difficulties with inconsistent supply and rigid dealer policies from other brands, Ajanta's dealer stood out for being supportive and easy to work with. Even during times of delayed payments, they never withheld material. That kind of support really helped us keep our work going smoothly. On top of that, Ajanta always gave us **steady quality and fair rates**, which made it easier for us to plan, produce, and grow our business with confidence.

This trust-based relationship with Ajanta gave us stability at a time when we needed it most.

Today, Mohan's is a trusted and respected brand, offering a wide range of high-quality products including biscuits, namkeen, toast, puffs, sweets, and snacks. Our strong market presence is a direct result of our dedication to excellence. Despite rising competition, we continue to prioritize quality above all.

As our operations scaled, our **partnership with Ajanta evolved into a long-term collaboration**, not just a supplier relationship. Their ability to meet our growing demand while maintaining product consistency helped us keep pace with our market expansion.

Our reach has expanded internationally, with exports to Australia, New Zealand, and Canada. Domestically, we serve markets across Uttar Pradesh, Delhi, Bihar, Punjab, Haryana, Rajasthan, Jammu & Kashmir, and Uttarakhand. We regularly launch new products under our tagline: Create, Bake, and Taste—a philosophy that reflects our belief that dedication and perseverance can overcome any challenge.

The bakery industry has evolved significantly over the years. We have embraced technology, replacing manual processes with advanced ovens and automated machinery. Through consistent effort and strategic growth and the support of partners like Ajanta, we have transformed from a small bakery into a large-scale operation.

We value customer feedback and use it to refine our offerings. Today, Mohan's is known for its unique specialties such as

Mohan's Milk Atta Patti, Mohan's Gud Atta Patti, Elaichi Rusk, Donut Cake, Spice Cake Fruit, Choco Chip Cake, Mohan's Son Papdi, Rasgulla, Gulabjamun, Bombay Mixture, Dry Slice Cake and Namkeens. With over 200 products in our portfolio, our journey stands as a testament to our commitment to quality, innovation, and customer satisfaction.

Behind every strong brand is a network of reliable partners. For us, Ajanta has been one of those pillars.

"जो साथ चलता है बिना शर्तों के,
वही असली साथी कहलाता है,
अजन्ता से रिश्ता हमारा सिर्फ़ व्यापार नहीं,
एक परिवार जैसा नाता है।"

– मनमोहन शर्मा

REFLECTION ACTIVITY

Reflect, Relate, Rise

These stories aren't just inspiring; they're real. Each one shows that the path to growth is filled with challenges, decisions, and the power of choosing the right partners. Now it's your turn to reflect and act.

Which part of these stories resonated with you the most and why?

If your journey was turned into a success story, what would its headline be?

So, when are you going to join the Ajanta Family?

Wait, Wait, Wait… There's Something More

I'm sharing this book because I want to see you succeed, and that means more than just words on a page.

So, on the next page, you'll find a special bonus chapter (especially for distributors) — advice and insights that could change the game for you.

This one's for you. Don't miss it.

CHAPTER 8

BULLETPROOFING YOUR DISTRIBUTION BUSINESS

"Take the stones people throw at you and use them to build a monument."
– Ratan Tata

Why Most Distributors Fail to Grow

The most common mistake a distribution business owner makes is constantly chasing new customers. Initially, this approach is necessary for survival, and often, it brings early success. However, what gets missed is that after a certain scale, it becomes crucial to ensure that existing customers are well-connected and well-serviced before you take the next big leap.

What we've observed is that while new customers are being chased, old customers are often ignored.

What needs to be understood:

Whatever is happening with your old customers will eventually happen with the new ones too.

Solution

Make a list of all the customers you've served till date and check how many are still active. Most people are shocked when they see the actual numbers.

If you're still serving 80% of your lifetime customer list, you're doing a great job — keep going.

But if that number is less than 30%, connect with each one — not to sell, but simply to understand what went wrong and why they stopped doing business with you.

Lack of Marketing Tools

For most people in distribution, marketing simply means sending out a salesperson to educate and convince the customer. Some take it further by using posters, danglers, or celebrity endorsements but that's still not the complete picture.

Marketing and sales are different — in both their goals and their efforts.

Today, digital marketing is commonly mistaken as the full definition of marketing, but it's just one form of it.

In simple words:

Marketing is the art of getting a YES from a customer at every stage — from being a stranger to becoming a fan.

To achieve this, you need the right tools and strategies at every step.

So always strive to present your product/service in a way that the other person feels eager to buy or at least move to the next step in their buying journey.

How to Ensure Long-Term, Profitable Growth

Another major struggle is ensuring consistent, long-term, profitable growth. Here are the three main reasons this doesn't happen:

1. Having a short-term mindset
2. Frequently switching companies/brands to distribute (being purely opportunistic)
3. Not being truly *useful* to your customer in a way that sets you apart

Understanding the Margin Game

Eventually, every distributor reaches a stage where margins become unattractive and too many players start selling the same product, further reducing profit levels.

This is natural. Wherever margins are high, more players enter — and this increased competition brings the margins down. This cycle happens in every industry.

So, what can you do?

Play the Long Game

Find and focus on **exclusive products** — ones where the company is genuinely committed to long-term growth. Build a strong, mutually beneficial relationship, and do justice to each other's efforts.

There will be hard times — but that's the real test of both sides:

How strong and committed are you to growing together?

Balancing Price and Value

If you are currently selling products where margins have shrunk to an uncomfortable level, don't panic or take drastic action. Instead, gradually start building high-margin product variants alongside your existing work.

Here's a powerful insight:

When you sell a price-sensitive (or cheap) product, you attract price-sensitive customers. These customers will always keep looking for cheaper alternatives, leading to low or no loyalty.

On the other hand, high-value and high-margin products attract quality-conscious customers. They are fewer in number, but they're loyal and happy to pay for the quality they get.

Yes, the market for such products may be smaller — but that's where the long-term wins lie. The world is clearly moving toward better quality ingredients and products in every space. So, continue running your current business but shift your focus and energy toward high-value, high-margin, quality products.

Most people lack this foresight — but those who build it will lead.

Being Useful Is the Best Marketing Tool

Being useful is the most powerful marketing tool one can use.

If you are consistently helpful to your customer and in a way that exceeds what your competitors offer — they don't stand a chance. You will always win.

Think about a recent product or service you purchased either for yourself or your business.

- Did you choose the cheapest option?

  Most likely, **no.**

- Did you choose the best one?

  You might say **yes**, but deep down, you know there are probably better products or services out there — ones you may or may not be aware of.

In most cases, you likely chose the person or brand who was more useful to you, someone who helped you understand, decide, or feel more confident about the purchase.

Even if, for some reason (maybe due to budget or availability), you didn't buy from them this time — if the situation allows, you'd prefer to buy from them next time. Why?

Because they were genuinely useful to you and that creates trust.

There will naturally be some challenges while implementing the above principles but they are absolutely possible to overcome.

For those who are connected with Ajanta, the process often becomes smoother, simply because there's a system of support in place.

That said, whether you're associated with us or not, these principles hold true. They can benefit your business — whether you're a distributor, a baker, or anyone working in this space.

REFLECTION ACTIVITY

What's Holding You Back?

Take a few minutes to reflect on the challenges you face in your own bakery or food business.

☑ What's relevant? Tick it:

- ☐ I've lost old customers while focusing on getting new ones.
- ☐ My margins are shrinking, and price wars are making it hard to sustain.
- ☐ I've never really introduced high-margin or value-added products in my business.
- ☐ I'm not regularly in touch with customers unless there's an issue.

Question:

If your top 5 customers were asked, "What makes you different from other distributors?" –

What do you hope they'll say? Write your answer here:

REFERENCES

1. **Wilmington, Delaware. (2024). Margarine Market. Allied Market Research**

   [Source: https://www.globenewswire.com/news-release/2024/08/19/2932123/0/en/Margarine-Market-to-Reach-29-2-Billion-Globally-by-2033-at-2-9-CAGR-Allied-Market-Research.html]

EXPERT TIPS FROM INDUSTRY LEADERS

Baking Basics: Smart Starts for New Bakers

1. Observe experienced bakers first, then practice with hands-on work.
2. Make unique items like flaxseed biscuits to stand out in the market.
3. Always check ingredients—especially oil—for freshness and smell.
4. While preparing cream, maintain the right temperature and mix water and oil properly.
5. Dilute essence in water before adding it to cream.
6. Display your finished items attractively to enhance appeal.
7. Choose fats that suit your product needs. While butter and cream offer rich flavor, specialty bakery fats like Frolic or vanaspati provide better shelf life, consistency, and volume
8. Avoid using GMS (Glycerine Monostearate), as it doesn't melt at body temperature and is harmful.
9. Choose creams that melt below 37°C for better digestibility.
10. For soft biscuits, use low melting point refined oil or quality ghee. For crispy biscuits, use eggs or eggless premix gel.
11. Use ingredients from reputed, trusted brands.
12. Desi ghee gives biscuits a soft texture and better health benefits

due to its low melting point.

13. In hot weather, store ghee in the freezer a day before use for better results.
14. Spray a mixture of water, oil, honey, and milk on puffs or cookies before baking to enhance shine and golden color.
15. Maintain hygiene—always wear caps and gloves while working.

Expert Edge: Tips to Level Up Your Bakery Game

1. Match dough consistency with the state of the ghee: hard ghee needs firm dough; soft ghee needs soft dough.
2. Use more ghee in patties and less in fan-style pastries.
3. Offer variety in patty fillings based on local taste—not just potato and cheese.
4. Add 25–30g sugar per kg of flour in puff pastries for a beautiful golden crust.
5. For soft, melt-in-the-mouth biscuits, reduce ammonia use and instead increase fat to 600–700g per kg of flour.
6. Understand how ghee and dough respond to oven heat—balance both to avoid uneven texture or collapse.

CONCLUSION & ACTION PLAN

Key Takeaways from the Book

1. **Quality Over Quantity:**

   In the bakery business, using premium oils and fats leads to better taste, texture, and shelf life, which directly boosts customer satisfaction. While cheaper oils may save money initially, they often compromise quality and consistency, resulting in long-term losses.

2. **Precision Equals Profitability:**

   Consistent oil and fat usage ensures that every batch tastes the same, building trust with your customers. By standardizing measurements and controlling portion sizes, you can reduce waste and improve your margins.

3. **Storage Makes a Difference:**

   Proper storage of oils and fats prevents spoilage and extends shelf life. Storing them in cool, dry places and using airtight containers keeps them fresh for longer, reducing waste and protecting your investment.

4. **Smarter Distribution, Less Waste:**

   Controlling oil distribution with measured dispensers and stock tracking reduces spillage and pilferage. By keeping a close eye on inventory, you minimize losses and maximize profitability.

5. **Adaptation Is Key to Growth:**

   The bakery industry is evolving with healthier alternatives and eco-friendly practices. Staying updated with low-trans-fat options and sustainable ingredients will help you meet customer demands and stay competitive.

Checklist for Bakers & Distributors

For Bakers:

1. **Daily Oil Measurement**
   - Use standardized measuring cups/ladles for all oil dispensing
   - Maintain a daily oil usage log (opening stock + usage + closing stock)
2. **Storage Optimization**
   - Store oils in cool, dark place (18-22°C ideal)
   - Use airtight containers with clear expiry date labels
   - Keep storage area locked with limited access
3. **Quality Control**
   - Conduct weekly taste tests comparing to standard samples
   - Implement monthly deep cleaning of all oil storage areas
   - Check oil quality before use (color, smell, consistency)
4. **Staff Training**
   - Conduct bi-weekly measurement technique refreshers
   - Display oil handling guidelines in prep areas
   - Assign oil management responsibilities to specific staff
   - Avoid baker monopoly – train and nurture chefs but

always have a second line ready to prevent taste disruption if they leave

5. **Cost Optimization**
    - Compare prices from 3 suppliers every quarter
    - Implement "oil-saving" idea box for staff suggestions
    - Review recipes monthly for oil efficiency improvements

For Distributors:

1. **Customer Education**
    - Create simple oil usage guides for different bakery products
    - Conduct quarterly demonstration sessions for clients
    - Share success stories from other bakeries
2. **Inventory Management**
    - Maintain buffer stock of fast-moving items; order what is sold, no guesswork
    - Implement first-expiry-first-out system
    - Conduct surprise quality checks on warehouse stock
3. **Value-Added Services**
    - Offer free oil storage containers with bulk orders
    - Provide monthly usage reports to regular clients
    - Develop customized oil blends for specific bakery needs, along with tips, recipes, and service insights that help clients boost their profits—everyone wants to feel special.
4. **Relationship Building**
    - Remember client preferences and special occasions
    - Check in with top clients bi-weekly
    - Create loyalty programs for consistent buyers and their

chefs—don't always sell, build relationships beyond business.

You could be an expert in something that solves their personal problem, they will value you for that.

5. **Market Awareness**
   - Stay updated on new oil/fat technologies
   - Monitor competitor offerings quarterly
   - Adjust product mix based on seasonal demands

A PERSONAL NOTE

First of all, thank you for taking the time to read this book. It truly means a lot to me.

While writing, I often wondered, "How will this impact the readers? Will they find it valuable?" Although the book is heavily focused on bakery businesses, it's not limited to them. Throughout the process, I kept thinking about how these insights could benefit other food businesses as well.

This book is the result of years of hands-on experience, and my goal was to create something that anyone in the food industry could use as a trusted companion. Whether you're a baker, distributor, or food entrepreneur, you'll find practical tips and strategies that can help you grow and succeed.

I would genuinely love to hear from you. You'll find my email ID in the next section—feel free to drop me a message sharing your thoughts, feedback, or even how this book has helped you.

Once again, thank you for being part of this journey. Wishing you success and growth in your business!

THE SOUL BEHIND AJANTA

This book would be incomplete without acknowledging my team, who hold a very special place in my heart.

I sincerely thank each and every member of the Ajanta family, both front-end and back-end, especially those from the bakery division, the plant, and the office.

I wanted to mention the names of every individual, past and present, who has been an integral part of Ajanta's journey and success. However, it would have been a gigantic mistake on my part to name only a few because in the end, it has always been a team effort. Some play leading roles, others contribute through technical expertise, but what I truly want to say is that *each one of you matters.* Like the fingers of a hand, unequal in shape, yet equally essential.

I thank you not only on behalf of the management but also from the bottom of my heart. I learn something new from you every day, and I sincerely wish for all of us to achieve even greater success in the times ahead.

Our channel partners are the true pillars and strength of Ajanta. Your loyalty and dedication make you much more than just distributors; you are true partners.

We look forward to working together for generations to come, and I hope to keep adding value to your lives, both personally and professionally.

THANK YOU FOR CHOOSING US!

We truly live by these words, and we are genuinely grateful to everyone who has chosen us.

Your trust is our strength.

LET'S BUTTER UP YOUR PROFITS!

You now hold the recipe for a more profitable bakery business—but why stop here? Let's make it even better!

- **Bakers:** Need help picking the right oils or fine-tuning your recipes? Let's create fluffier, tastier, and more consistent products.
- **Distributors:** Want to become the go-to supplier for quality fats? Let me help you offer premium solutions your clients will love.
- **Business Owners:** Looking to cut waste, boost margins, and grow sustainably? Let's strategize together.

Got doubts, ideas, or need expert guidance?

I'm here to help! You can schedule a 1-on-1 meeting with me, and I assure you that I'll guide you in the best possible way. Together, we can unlock new opportunities and drive your business towards greater success.

Don't wait—start small, test smart, and scale big.

Abhey Goyal

Scan this QR to leave feedback or get in touch to address your specific challenges, explore strategies relevant to your needs and pave the way for your growth.

Email: *hello@abheygoyal.com*

Website: *www.abheygoyal.com*